SHIFT

A Journey to Awaken Purpose, Power, and Impact

Shirley A. Amanfo

SHIFT

Copyright ©2025 **Shirley A. Amanfo**
Paperback ISBN: 978-1-965593-56-1

All rights reserved. No part of this publication may be reproduced, distributed, or transmitted in any form or by any means, including photocopying, recording, or other electronic or mechanical methods without the prior written permission of the author except in the case of brief quotations embodied in reviews and certain other non-commercial uses permitted by copyright law.

Published by Cornerstone Publishing

A Division of Cornerstone Creativity Group LLC
Info@thecornerstonepublishers.com
www.thecornerstonepublishers.com

Author's Contact

To book the author to speak at your next event or to order bulk copies of this book, please, use the information below:

info@shirleyamanfo.com | shirleyamanfo.com

Printed in the United States of America.

FOREWORD

This book, SHIFT, is a compelling call to rise above mediocrity and embrace the full measure of your Godgiven potential. Shirley makes a powerful appeal that persuades the reader that we were made for more, that God's plan is for us to lead and transform the world by unleashing all we carry within.

This book will help you finalize your divorce from excuses and position you with a fresh focus and faith to overcome life's challenges. It will open your eyes to the truth that hardship often holds the key to your strength. It will call forth value, productivity, and kingdom-driven results.

Don't worry about lost time or past delays. As you encounter the truths in these pages, you'll begin to feel time redeem itself as clarity and courage return. Even pain can become purposeful and profitable when you apply the principles found here.

I encourage you to open your heart and adopt a mindset of "whatever it takes." As you read on, you will be reminded of your authority as a believer. May miracles, wisdom, and bold leadership mark your journey, and may your legacy be a shining witness to generations.

Happy reading,

Apostle Dr. Joy Jones
President & Founder,
Life Changers Club International

DEDICATION

To those still seeking their purpose in life. May you find clarity, strength, and courage to walk confidently in your divine calling.

Also, to my beloved husband, Eddy, and our wonderful family. Being surrounded by all of you makes life's journey truly spectacular. "Behold, how delightful and advantageous it is for brothers to dwell in harmony."
Psalm 133:1 (NLT)

ACKNOWLEDGMENTS

All glory to God—my source of strength, wisdom, and grace. This book is the result of His guidance, and I am His vessel.

To my husband, Edwin, thank you for your unwavering love and belief in me. To our children, Michelle, Jennifer, Jordan, and Gabby, your joy, encouragement, and patience have been my daily fuel.

To my parents and Pastors Ayo and Layide Ajayi, your steadfast prayers and wisdom continue to shape and uplift me. Thank you for investing in my spiritual growth.

To my early reviewers, Dr. John Ojo, Mr. Chidi Chinke, and Pastor Shola Adegoke, thank you for your time, thoughtful feedback, and encouragement.

To my coach and mentor, Lady Vivian Jokotade, your guidance from the very beginning gave this book its voice. From a one-page outline to a fully reimagined manuscript, your wisdom, critique, and clarity on tone and title were instrumental. You helped shape this book into what it was truly meant to be.

To Apostle Tomi Arayomi and the Goshen community, your powerful teaching and tools stirred something in me. Thank you for helping me overcome delays and finish strong.

To Apostle Dr. Joy Jones, thank you for writing a compelling foreword that brought life to this work. Even when the manuscript was still rough, you saw the vision. Your affirmation meant more than you know.

And to my friends, editors, and silent champions, your fingerprints are woven into every chapter. I am deeply grateful.

CONTENTS

Preface..10

The Power of One Shift...15

1. Awakening the Resilient Mind..18
2. Breaking Barriers: How to Overcome Excuses and Delays..24
3. Reclaiming Opportunities: Conquering Ignorance & Fear...30
4. The Creative Power of Thoughts and Words.................38
5. Mastering Stress: Winning the Battle in Your Mind......44
6. From Rebellion to Redemption: Walking in Authority..50
7. Unleashing Your Divine Authority Through Creativity...56
8. Christianity Vs. Legalism: Embracing True Freedom....62
9. The Discipline of Diligence: Overcoming Idleness for Growth..68
10. Faithful Living: The Path to Success & Increase............74
11. Persistence & Profit: Thriving Through Faithfulness....80

12. The Graveyard of Greatness: How to Avoid Wasted Potential..86

13. Beyond Survival: Thriving in God's Calling..................92

14. Building A Legacy: Turning Purpose into Daily Action..98

15. Mastering Life's Seasons: Thriving in Every Stage........104

16. The Power of Discipleship: Walking in Kingdom Authority..113

Epilogue...117

References..121

PREFACE

This book began as a whisper, a nudge from God in a season where I was caught between responsibility and identity. I was succeeding on the outside, but silently questioning my pace, my peace, and my purpose. In that quiet tension, I sensed God asking me to shift, not into busyness, but into alignment.

I started writing in fragments: journal entries, voice memos, ideas on napkins, and bedside notes. Slowly, it came together—not as a manual for perfection but as a blueprint for boldness. This book is not about doing more. It's about becoming more rooted in your assignment and more aware of the authority God has given you.

SHIFT is the message I needed when I felt overwhelmed and underutilized. I hope that it will serve as a companion for anyone navigating transition, waiting for clarity, or longing for a breakthrough.

If you've ever felt stuck between what is and what could be, this book is for you.

THE JOURNEY AHEAD

A four-part path of personal growth, purpose, and impact.

This book unfolds in four distinct parts; each one intentionally designed to guide you from self-awareness to spiritual authority, from burnout to boldness, from hesitation to legacy. As you journey through these pages, allow each section to meet you where you are and gently lead you forward.

PART 1: FOUNDATIONS OF SHIFTING
Chapters 1–4

This section is your soul's ignition point. As you open these pages, you'll step into the gentle but firm invitation to shift out of performance and into purpose, out of fear and into faith. It's about laying down the weight of "doing" and picking up the grace of "becoming." These chapters awaken awareness, initiate healing, and call forth the courage to begin your transformation.

PART 2: BUILDING RESILIENT IDENTITY
Chapters 5–7

Now that the shift has begun, this section helps you dig deeper. These chapters are about recovering your God-given identity and embracing divine timing. You'll break free from comparison, shake off fear, and reclaim your authority. This is where boldness rises—not because you have it all figured out, but because you finally know who you are.

PART 3: DISCIPLINE & DILIGENCE FOR GROWTH
Chapters 8–11

Here, we move from identity to execution. These chapters explore the habits, mindset, and strategies needed to grow, build, and multiply what's in your hands. You'll learn to steward time with purpose, work with excellence, and embrace persistence as a spiritual principle. Growth isn't just a goal, it's your responsibility.

PART 4: LEGACY & KINGDOM INFLUENCE
Chapters 12–17

This final section brings it all together. Now that you've shifted inwardly and begun to build outwardly, it's time to think generationally. These chapters challenge you to live for legacy, mentor others, and thrive in every season of life. This is where impact begins—not with perfection, but with obedience and vision. Your life is a seed, and what you do with it will echo beyond your lifetime.

THE POWER OF ONE SHIFT

Before you begin...

Look for the one gentle nudge; God's whisper that leads not to revolution, but to transformation. This introduction reminds you: one shift is more than enough.

INTRODUCTION

THE POWER OF ONE SHIFT

Have you ever had a moment where something inside you quietly whispered, "This can't be it"? Not a breakdown. Not a loud cry for help. Just a subtle pause, a sacred nudge—that made you wonder if there was more within you than what life had allowed to bloom so far.

I remember such a moment clearly. I wasn't falling apart, but I wasn't thriving either. I was functioning, meeting expectations, showing up, pushing through. But inside, I was running on fumes, emotionally depleted, and spiritually distant from the strength I knew I once carried. That was the day I realized I didn't need a revolution. I needed a shift. Not a dramatic reinvention. Just one change—one thought reframed, one habit reexamined, one burden laid down. And that one shift became the seed of a new mindset. A more resilient one. A gentler one. A mindset rooted not in perfection or performance, but in grace, awareness, and slow but steady transformation.

This book is an invitation. Not to fix everything overnight. Not to become a new person in a week. But to begin. To embrace the process of becoming resilient, not in a loud, aggressive way, but in quiet courage. One step at a time. One thought at a time. One shift at a time.

We don't arrive at resilience. We grow into it. You don't need to force it. You're not late. You haven't missed your moment.

You're shifting, and that's more than enough.

AWAKENING THE RESILIENT MIND

Step in, ready to discover...

How quiet resilience begins—not with force, but with a shift. See resistance in a new light, and embrace your authority.

CHAPTER 1
AWAKENING THE RESILIENT MIND

"God blessed them and said to them, 'Be fruitful and increase in number; fill the earth and subdue it. Rule over the fish in the sea and the birds in the sky and over every living creature that moves on the ground." —Genesis 1:28 (NIV)

THE PAUSE THAT SHIFTED EVERYTHING

I remember sitting in my car one afternoon, the engine off, keys still in hand, but I wasn't going anywhere. My eyes were fixed on the dashboard, but my mind was scattered in a thousand directions, emails waiting, travel plans to confirm, meetings stacked one after the other. And somehow, amid that spinning mental to-do list, I realised I had hit an invisible wall.

I wasn't burned out in the way people often say, I could still function, still produce, still show up, but somewhere between doing and being, I had drifted. I was showing up for everyone but not present to myself. That day, I didn't fall apart—I paused long enough to hear a whisper: "There has to be more."

I didn't need a new calendar or a fresh strategy. I needed a shift. Just a small one. A shift in mindset. In belief. In breath. That moment marked the beginning of something more profound—a gentle, awakening to a type of strength that doesn't shout but remains. A quiet resilience that holds you together when everything else feels like it's falling apart.

THE TREADMILL REVELATION

Not long after, I stepped onto my home treadmill, ready to move forward again, literally and figuratively. I had imagined this scene so clearly: confident strides, a soundtrack of motivation, endorphins rising.

But instead, I stumbled. Hard. Fell right off the thing.

My pride took the biggest hit. I sat there on the floor, questioning everything. "Maybe I'm not cut out for this." But a different thought gently interrupted: "What if falling isn't the failure, what if quitting is?"

So, I got back on. Slowly this time. I adjusted. I found a rhythm that worked. I didn't sprint, but I didn't stop either. That treadmill taught me what books and podcasts couldn't. That strength is built in the tension. That failure can be part of the lesson. That resilience doesn't always roar—sometimes, it simply returns.

FINDING STRENGTH IN SCRIPTURE

The Bible isn't just filled with miracle moments; it is full of stories of people who wrestled, waited, and walked through long roads of resistance. There's the story of two scouts: Joshua and Caleb. They were sent to spy out the Promised Land. Ten others returned, overwhelmed by the giants they saw, but Joshua and Caleb saw the possibility. Their faith didn't ignore the facts; it simply trusted in a bigger God (Numbers 13).

Jacob, who later became Israel, wrestled with God through the night. He didn't come away untouched; he limped. But that limp was also his mark of transformation. He had met God in his struggle, and it changed everything (Genesis 32).

Tamar, a lesser-known woman in Scripture, refused to let cultural shame and injustice define her. She took a bold and unconventional stand to preserve her family's lineage. Her son Perez would go on to be part of the genealogy that led to Jesus (Genesis 38). That's how redemptive God is. He weaves even pain into purpose.

FROM LEGACY TO MODERN HEROES

Resilience isn't just a biblical trait. It echoes through history. Harriet Tubman didn't just run toward freedom. She turned back repeatedly, risking her life to help others escape slavery. Her story reminds us that true resilience isn't just about surviving, it's about lifting others as you go.

Maya Angelou, silenced for years by trauma, found her voice in poetry and speech that awakened generations. Her pain didn't disappear, but it became her platform.

Even someone like Jerry Seinfeld. Yes, the comedian, once bombed so badly on stage he questioned everything. But he got back up, returned, and refined. That consistent resilience built a legacy of laughter.

These stories, biblical and modern, remind us that resilience doesn't always wear a cape. Sometimes, it wears yesterday's disappointment and still shows up for today's purpose.

A RESILIENT IDENTITY

Scripture calls us "a chosen generation, a royal priesthood" (1 Peter 2:9). That's not poetic fluff, it's a divine reminder: You were not created to shrink back. You were born to rise, to rebuild, to reign.

Even when you don't feel strong, even when the week has drained you, you still carry the imprint of God's authority. Colossians 1:13 tells us we've been transferred, not temporarily relocated but permanently repositioned into the Kingdom of light.

James adds another layer: trials are tools. They produce perseverance. And perseverance completes us (James 1:2-4). So, the very thing you think is wearing you down might be the thing God is using to build you up.

What Happens When You Shift?

- You stop waiting for ideal circumstances and start owning your identity.
- You stop seeing resistance as a wall and begin seeing it as a training ground.
- You stop chasing perfection and start honoring progress.
- Because strength isn't proven when life is easy, it's revealed when life is hard, and you rise anyway.

Reflection Prompt:

- Where in your life have you felt weary, stuck, or unsure?
- What slight shift of mindset, of trust, of action, could mark the beginning of your next breakthrough?

BREAKING BARRIERS

Get set to move...

Excuses may sound reasonable, but they cost you. This chapter invites you to take your first brave step in faith.

CHAPTER 2

BREAKING BARRIERS: HOW TO OVERCOME EXCUSES AND DELAYS

"Whatever you do, work at it with all your heart, as working for the Lord... knowing that you will receive an inheritance from the Lord as a reward."
—*Colossians 3:23-24 (NIV)*

WHEN EXCUSES WEAR A DISGUISE

Have you ever caught yourself offering what sounded like wisdom, but felt more like hesitation wrapped in spiritual sincerity? "I'm just being cautious," we say. Or: "It's not the right season yet." These statements often sound responsible until we realize they're excuses masquerading as caution.

Take Jasper, for instance. A seasoned broker, he'd prepared meticulously for a career-defining interview. The night before, he prayed, he rehearsed, he envisioned success. But on the morning of the interview, a sudden road closure stalled him for nearly an hour. Despite leaving an apologetic voicemail, the opportunity passed him by—no bitter betrayal, just life moving forward as he was held back. That day taught him—and reminds me daily—that even the most reasonable delay can derail a dream.

PURPOSE DOESN'T WAIT FOR PERFECT TIMING

Imagine if every emergency medical team decided they'd wait for ideal conditions before responding. The patient could die in those precious minutes. Yet, we let our purpose wait for perfect clarity, timing, or a green light that never seems to come.

When the Israelites faced the Red Sea, blocked by water on one side and an army on the other, their instinct was fear. Moses was told to act: "Go forward!" The water didn't part while they hesitated, they opened as they walked. Sometimes, the miracle we seek is waiting on our movement, not our comfort.

LEAP OF FAITH: THE TEXAS MOVE

I recall the doubts that shadowed our family when we discussed moving from Arizona to Texas. We wondered aloud: Would we find jobs? Could we afford the change? Was this God's direction?

Then one afternoon, a Steve Harvey clip played "accidentally" on my phone. He spoke about people stuck in a helicopter, waiting for the proper signal to jump. He warned that waiting for perfect clarity usually means never jumping at all. His words felt like God speaking, so clear I couldn't ignore them.

We moved. The clarity came after commitment. Texas turned out not to be a gamble—it was the next stride we needed to take.

EXTRAORDINARY LIVES, ORDINARY BEGINNINGS

It's easy to look at success and forget that beginnings matter. Nick Vujicic, born without arms or legs, once believed he had no future. Yet today, he inspires millions to dream despite limitations.

Michael Jordan was cut from his high school team. That moment could have defined him. Instead, it pushed him to train harder, and he became one of the greatest athletes of all time. His cut became his catalyst.

And then there's J.K. Rowling, writing her manuscript in cafés while a single mom is on government aid. Rejected by multiple publishers, she could have stopped, but she didn't. Her faith and her pen kept moving—and today, the world knows her name.

They all faced delays when excuses could've taken root. But they refused to let delays become destiny.

THE POWER OF THE FIRST STEP

So, what if you don't have a five-year plan? What if you only have a flicker of conviction, a nudge in your heart? That's enough.

I once began drafting a business proposal late at night—no launch date, no investors, just one page of ideas. It wasn't perfect, but it was a start. That page later became a project that grew into something bigger than I could have planned.

Momentum isn't built on leaps alone. It's born in small, consistent steps.

What Happens When You Shift?

When you choose movement over perfection:

- Excuses lose their charm.
- Your purpose, however whispered, begins to breathe.
- Holy momentum steps into your daily rhythm.
- Your soul wakes up to what faith and action together can birth.

Reflection Prompt:

- What "wise excuse" have you embraced—waiting for clarity, more time, or better conditions?
- What's one small move you can make today—an email, a phone call, a draft, to break the delay and step toward your conviction?

RECLAIMING OPPORTUNITIES

Listen for doors opening...

Fear and ignorance can keep you from your destiny. Here, you'll find the courage to move forward into new spaces.

CHAPTER 3

RECLAIMING OPPORTUNITIES: CONQUERING IGNORANCE & FEAR

"My people are destroyed from lack of knowledge."
—Hosea 4:6 (NIV)

THE ROOM THAT ALMOST INTIMIDATED ME

I didn't discover the opportunity through a carefully planned workshop or a personal invitation. It showed up the way many things do these days—on Instagram. The NP Elite group kept appearing in my feed, and each time, something in me leaned in with interest. But alongside that curiosity came a wave of second-guessing.

"It's probably for people way ahead of me."

"They're already building empires."

I'm just figuring things out."

"I don't have the money or time."

Nothing on the outside disqualified me, but my inner voice nearly did. I hadn't been told "no." I had quietly told myself I wasn't enough. But in the quiet swirl of that tension, I sensed God's nudge: "Say yes. You'll grow into the room." So, I did. I joined. And the doors that opened were more than I could have planned. I found not only education and exposure, but also a deep sense of alignment. The questions I carried found answers, and the fears I had were met with support, clarity, and a sense of momentum.

THE QUIET THIEF CALLED IGNORANCE

Ignorance doesn't always look like absence, it often looks like hesitation, delay, or playing small. Sometimes we think we're protecting ourselves with caution, when we're keeping ourselves from the very spaces where growth could occur.

The Bible speaks plainly: "My people are destroyed for lack of knowledge." (Hosea 4:6) It doesn't say they perished for lack of love, prayer, or intention. The issue was knowledge, clarity, insight, and awareness.

It's the scholarship that I never applied for because someone assumed I wouldn't qualify. It's the promotion that was not pursued because someone feared being misunderstood.

It's the calling ignored because someone thought they needed to be more "ready."

Real knowledge isn't about collecting data. It's about understanding that leads to movement—awareness that ignites transformation.

FROM ESTHER TO EVERYDAY TRAILBLAZERS

Consider Esther. She didn't grow up royal. She was a young Jewish woman in exile, raised by her cousin, Mordecai. Yet when the time came to risk everything for her people, she leaned into courage; not because she had a master plan, but because she trusted God and listened to wise counsel. Her story reminds us that preparation isn't always external, it's often about positioning your heart.

Or think about David. He wasn't trained as a warrior. He was a shepherd boy, tending sheep and playing music. But when a giant threatened his people, he stepped forward— not with armor, but with a sling, a testimony, and an unshakable confidence in God. He won, not because he was the most qualified, but because he refused to let fear lead the narrative.

In today's world, the same pattern holds.

Malala Yousafzai didn't start with a global platform, just a passion for education and the courage to speak out. Sara

Blakely wasn't handed a business degree. She started with an idea and a relentless drive to solve a problem. Simone Biles didn't arrive at greatness overnight, she showed up consistently, pushing through setbacks, refining her craft. None of them waited to feel perfect. They responded to an inner knowing that said, "Start anyway."

WHEN THE "Aha" MOMENT COMES

Sometimes, God answers our prayers not with fireworks, but with insight. That "aha" moment—where clarity clicks and everything falls into place- can be a quiet invitation into something more.

The book of Joel contains this powerful promise: "I will restore to you the years the locusts have eaten." (Joel 2:25) Restoration isn't passive; it is partnered with response. When God begins restoring, He also begins instructing.

A woman I mentored once felt completely boxed in by her job. She was gifted, capable, but uninspired. Instead of quitting in frustration, she started researching. She attended free webinars. She found a coach. Slowly, she began designing a life that reflected her values. She didn't wait for everything to be clear. She moved in the direction of the nudge, and the next steps unfolded as she went.

MINDSET SHIFT = OPPORTUNITY SHIFT

Many people leave bondage, but never leave the mindset of bondage. That was the case with the Israelites. They escaped Egypt, but Egypt still lingered in their thoughts. They feared scarcity, doubted their leadership, and often yearned to return to the very place they'd prayed to leave.

But Joshua and Caleb were different. They were among the twelve spies who scouted the Promised Land, and while others were intimidated by the giants, these two were anchored in God's promise. They saw a possibility where others saw a risk.

That's what happens when your mindset shifts. The same landscape looks different. Where others retreat, you press forward, not because fear is absent, but because faith has grown louder.

Faith Isn't About Having All the Answers Some of Jesus' most moving miracles came through people with no spiritual résumé—just bold faith.

One was a Gentile woman—an outsider—who begged Jesus to heal her daughter. Her persistence moved Him. He answered, "Woman, you have great faith!" and granted her request (Matthew 15:28).

Another was a Roman military officer who said, "Just speak the word, and my servant will be healed." His confidence in Jesus' authority was so remarkable that Jesus said He hadn't seen faith like that in all of Israel (Matthew 8:10).

These weren't scholars or leaders. They were regular people with extraordinary trust.

That same kind of faith lives in you.

What Happens When You Shift?

- You stop preemptively closing doors that God is inviting you through.
- Ignorance becomes fuel for discovery, not a reason to stay stuck.
- Fear quiets. Purpose becomes louder.
- Promise begins to meet action, because you choose to move.

Reflection Prompt:

- What opportunity have you quietly told yourself you're not ready for?
- What would it look like to say yes before you feel fully qualified?

THE CREATIVE POWER OF THOUGHTS

Ready for modern-day miracle-working?

Your words shape reality. This chapter will help you brace your thoughts and begin speaking life.

CHAPTER 4

THE CREATIVE POWER OF THOUGHTS AND WORDS

"The tongue has the power of life and death, and those who love it will eat its fruit." —Proverbs 18:21 (NIV)

THE STORIES WE TELL OURSELVES

She had the credentials. The quiet confidence. The potential. But sitting across from me that day, she confessed something that gripped me: "I keep sabotaging myself with the things I say in my head." She wasn't talking about outside criticism or toxic comments from others. She was referring to her inner voice—the one whispering things like: "I'm not good enough." "What if I mess this up?" "Who do I think I am to try this?"

And as I listened, I realized she's not alone. So many of us are fighting invisible battles with words we've allowed to take root. We believe our issue is related to time, resources, or confidence. But often, it starts with a simple, repeating thought we never confronted.

Before our words reach others, they echo in our minds. And what we speak—whether out loud or silently—carries creative power.

WHEN YOUR MIND IS THE GARDEN

Proverbs 18:21 is not metaphorical fluff, it's a blueprint: "The tongue has the power of life and death."

Your words aren't just sound waves, they're seeds. What you repeat, whether in faith or fear will grow.

The lame man at the Pool of Bethesda (John 5) illustrates this. When Jesus asked, "Do you want to be made well?" the man didn't answer with hope. He responded with limitation: "I have no one to help me."

His belief had become boxed in by experience. His healing came not just through physical touch, but through a mindset shift.

WHEN WORDS BECOME PATHWAYS OR PITFALLS

Ruth's story proves this, too. When faced with the choice to return to familiarity or press into the unknown, she declared: "Your God will be my God." That wasn't just loyalty. That was prophecy. Her words ushered her into a life of divine favor, redemption, and legacy.

Even science affirms this. Studies have shown that plants thrive in environments with affirming speech and wither in those with negative speech. If plants respond to words, imagine the impact on the human soul.

Romans 12:2 urges us to "be transformed by the renewing of your mind."

That renewal doesn't start with a big leap; it begins with what you tell yourself in quiet moments.

THE DAMAGE OF IDLE TALK

It's not just the inner dialogue we must watch—it's the careless, throwaway words we speak to others. Jesus warned, "You will give account for every idle word..." (Matthew 12:36). Paul echoed it: "Let no corrupt word proceed from your mouth, but only what is good for building others up..." (Ephesians 4:29). Gossip, sarcasm, passive-aggressive jabs—they don't just fill space. They shape culture, breed distrust, and fracture relationships.

REBUILDING WITH WORDS

Think of the relationships that crumbled from one harsh sentence—or those restored by a single, sincere apology. Words are bridges or barriers. They create safety or suspicion.

A compliment can heal. A cutting remark can undo years of trust.

In boardrooms and bedrooms, pulpits and playgrounds, our words either build or break. That's why Proverbs 15:28 tells us to "weigh our answers."

SPEAK LIFE ON PURPOSE

Jesus said it clearly: "Out of the abundance of the heart, the mouth speaks" (Luke 6:45). If our speech is sharp, perhaps our heart is sore. If our words are healing, it's likely because we've allowed God to heal us first.

The woman I spoke with that day? Her change didn't come through affirmation from others. It came the moment she caught herself mid-thought and chose a new sentence:

"I'm not a failure, I'm a learner."

"I'm not unqualified, I'm being equipped."

And that shift—though small, opened the door to transformation.

What Happens When You Shift?
- Your thoughts become allies instead of enemies.
- Your words build trust, healing, and vision in

every room you enter.
- You begin to declare who you are becoming, not just what you've experienced.

Reflection Prompt:
- What's one negative inner phrase you need to retire today?
- How can you intentionally speak life over yourself and others?

MASTERING STRESS

Step into your power under pressure...Stress doesn't have to break you—it can build you. Discover how preparation and faith make you stronger.

CHAPTER 5

MASTERING STRESS: WINNING THE BATTLE IN YOUR MIND

"I lie down and sleep; I wake again because the Lord sustains me. I will not fear though tens of thousands assail me on every side." —Psalm 3:5–6 (NIV)

THE NIGHT BEFORE MY NIH INTERVIEW

It was the night before one of the biggest interviews of my life—my first opportunity with the National Institutes of Health. While the world outside my window slept, my thoughts were wide awake. My mind played out every possible failure: What if I freeze? What if I forget my answers? What if I'm not enough?

Stress felt like a tidal wave. But somewhere in that swell of pressure, a quiet voice rose above the noise: You've prepared. You belong here. God is with you.

I didn't silence the anxiety by pretending it wasn't there. I confronted it with prayer, preparation, and perspective. I reminded myself of the path that had led me to this moment, and that the God who brought me here wouldn't leave me now.

That night taught me something powerful: stress doesn't have to be the enemy. Sometimes, it's the proving ground where our confidence is forged.

STRESS IS NOT ENEMY, AVOIDANCE IS

We often label stress as a villain, as something to eliminate. But what if we saw it differently?

James 1:2-4 urges us to "consider it pure joy... when you face trials," because those trials refine us. Stress, like fire, can burn or it can purify. The outcome depends on how we approach it.

Think of stress as a signal, not a sentence. It's alerting you to something that matters—something that needs your attention, growth, or surrender.

FROM PRESSURE TO PURPOSE

Kobe Bryant once said, "Everything negative–pressure, challenges–is all an opportunity for me to rise." His discipline wasn't driven by fear but by purpose. While others slept, he trained, not because he had to, but because he was committed to growing through the grind.

And that's what stress can be; a refining tool. Under pressure, we sharpen. We see what we're made of. We discover what matters. However, when stress goes unmanaged, it becomes more than just pressure—it becomes toxic.

Unchecked stress can cloud your clarity, drain your joy, and distort your perspective. That's why we don't just need to survive stress—we need to steward it.

JESUS DIDN'T AVOID PRESSURE, HE REFRAMED IT

Jesus never promised a life free of trouble. But He did promise peace that surpasses understanding (John 14:27). He modeled what it means to face stress with purpose.

In Gethsemane, He felt the full weight of pressure. He sweated blood, prayed earnestly, and still surrendered with, "Not my will, but Yours be done." That moment reminds us that even the Son of God experienced strain—and overcame it not by resistance, but by release.

PRACTICAL RHYTHMS FOR A RESILIENT MIND

So, how do we master stress instead of letting it master us? Here are five practical rhythms that realign your heart and habits:

- Prepare with intention. The unknown loses power when you show up ready. Preparation quiets panic.

- Reframe your mindset. Stress isn't punishment—it's potential. Look for what God is teaching in the tension.

- Lean into community. You were never meant to carry everything alone. Invite someone into your process.

- Care for your temple. Eat well. Move your body. Get rest. Physical health supports spiritual clarity.

- Stay rooted in God. Worship. Journal. Meditate on scripture. Let His truth anchors your swirling thoughts. And sometimes, the most spiritual thing you can do... is breathe, drink water, and whisper, "Lord, help me today."

What Happens When You Shift?

- You stop seeing stress as a threat and start seeing it as training.
- You become less reactive and more reflective.
- You build resilience that isn't loud, but lasting.

Reflection Prompt:

- How might God be using current stress to refine—not ruin—you?
- What's one shift you can make this week to steward pressure more intentionally?

FROM REBELLION TO REDEMPTION

Prepare to reclaim what was lost...

From Eden to the cross, your authority has been restored. Let this chapter ignite your confidence to walk in dominion.

CHAPTER 6

FROM REBELLION TO REDEMPTION: WALKING IN AUTHORITY

"But God demonstrates his love for us in this: While we were still sinners, Christ died for us." —Romans 5:8 (NIV)

THE DAY I LEARNED SURRENDER WAS STRENGTH

I used to think that surrender was a sign of weakness. That giving in meant giving up. That obedience would somehow dull the fire God placed in me. I wanted to make an impact, to carry influence—but without the discomfort of pruning or the weight of responsibility. Deep down, I feared that surrendering to God fully would cost me too much.

Then one quiet morning, I sat with my Bible and read Romans 5:8: "While we were still sinners, Christ died for us."

That verse silenced every argument in my head. Christ didn't wait for me to get it right. He died for me at my worst. That wasn't weakness—that was love. Power wrapped in mercy. And in that moment, something shifted. I stopped trying to earn authority and started living from the authority already restored through Christ.

EDEN: WHERE AUTHORITY BEGAN

In Eden, humanity walked in divine alignment—governing, naming, creating—while fully immersed in God's presence. Authority was never about domination; it was about stewardship in relationship with the Creator. As long as Adam and Eve stayed connected to God, they flourished. But when that connection was broken, authority fractured.

God's design was clear: dominion flows from intimacy.

WHEN REBELLION ENTERED THE STORY

Before the garden, before the fall, there was another rebellion.

Lucifer, once radiant with glory, allowed pride to twist his purpose. He didn't just want influence—he wanted God's throne. His rebellion cost him everything. Cast down from heaven, his rage turned toward humanity. If he couldn't rule in heaven, he would try to ruin God's image on earth.

In Eden, he slithered in subtly, not to overthrow Adam, but to whisper doubt. "Did God really say...?" It wasn't a blatant attack—it was an invitation to question the truth.

And it worked.

Eve reached. Adam stayed silent. Together, they surrendered their authority—not to a serpent, but to self. They lost Eden, not because of ignorance, but because of disobedience.

BUT REDEMPTION WAS ALREADY IN MOTION

Here's the miracle: before the first sin, God had already written the plan of salvation. Revelation 13:8 says the Lamb was slain before the foundation of the world. That means grace isn't a reaction—it's God's eternal posture toward us.

Satan thought he won a cosmic chess match. But God had already checkmated darkness with a cross and an empty tomb.

JESUS: THE SECOND ADAM, THE FINAL AUTHORITY

Romans 5:17 draws the contrast: through Adam, death reigned. But through Jesus, life reigns. Jesus didn't just forgive sin—He restored position. He reopened Eden.

Through the cross, Jesus reclaimed what was lost. And through His resurrection, He invites us to rule again—spiritually, purposefully, and in alignment with heaven.

This is not just forgiveness. It's reinstatement.

LIVING LIKE IT'S ALREADY RESTORED

Jesus said, "Apart from Me, you can do nothing" (John 15:5). Authority disconnected from God becomes performance. But authority connected to God becomes purpose.

When you stay in Christ, you don't have to chase validation. You walk in quiet confidence, knowing you've been placed, empowered, and sent.

DENZEL WASHINGTON: A MODERN-DAY REMINDER

We all know Denzel as a gifted actor. But behind the screen is a story of transformation. In 2024, he took a public step many wouldn't expect—he was baptized and ordained, declaring his full surrender to God's call.

That wasn't just about personal faith—it was about authority. It was about recognizing that true influence begins with submission.

Like Denzel, you may carry potential. But power comes when you let God refine it.

What Happens When You Shift?

- You stop seeing obedience as loss and start seeing it as access.
- You release performance and receive permission to walk, to lead, to reign.
- You remember, Eden isn't lost. It's been restored. And you are invited back in.

Reflection Prompt:

- Where in your life have you been hesitating to surrender because it feels like a loss?
- What could shift if you saw surrender as strength, and obedience as access to divine authority?

UNLEASHING YOUR DIVINE CREATIVITY

Tune in to something bigger...God's ideas flow through you. This chapter shows how intimacy sparks a breakthrough

CHAPTER 7

UNLEASHING YOUR DIVINE AUTHORITY THROUGH CREATIVITY

"So God created human beings in His image. In the image of God, He created them, male and female. Then God blessed them and said, 'Be fruitful and multiply. Fill the earth and govern it.'" —Genesis 1:27-28 (NLT)

WHEN CREATIVITY BECOMES A CONVERSATION WITH GOD

When I first opened my clinic, the dream felt like it had been heaven-sent. But the path? That part felt foggy. I knew I had the skills, the calling—but the daily decisions? The systems, the staffing, the finances? There were moments I stared at my planner or sat in silence, unsure of my next move.

Then, in the stillness—when I stopped striving and invited God in—ideas would flow. Ideas that no class had taught me. No mentor had suggested. Yet they fit perfectly. They weren't just good ideas—they were God's ideas. Solutions that carried peace. Insights that sparked progress. Arrangements in the waiting room calmed anxious patients. Outreach concepts that spoke to our community's heart.

I realized something sacred: creativity is not just a skill; it's a divine conversation.

DIVINE CREATIVITY: BEYOND IMAGINATION

You were made to create, not just for productivity, but for purpose. Genesis tells us that we're made in God's image. That means creativity is woven into your DNA. But divine creativity flows from intimacy.

Like Moses, who left God's presence with his face glowing, your time with God births things the world can't manufacture. Solutions, strategies, designs, and messages that change lives—they're not downloaded from hustle, but from heaven.

Imagine sitting with the Creator of the universe every morning and saying, "What do You want to build through me today?" That's what divine partnership looks like. It's not just inspiration—it's alignment.

CREATIVITY ALIGNED WITH PURPOSE

When creativity partners with calling, impact multiplies.

The Wright brothers weren't engineers. Marie Curie

didn't have today's labs. However, they pressed through limitations to reshape the course of history. Now imagine if they'd also leaned into divine wisdom. What happens when creativity isn't just human but heavenly?

It isn't distant. He's not withholding brilliance. He's waiting for communion. For someone to pause long enough to ask, listen, and act.

You don't need a stage or a title to create something that shifts atmospheres. Your idea, birthed in God's presence, could be the answer someone's been praying for.

PRACTICES THAT UNLOCK CREATIVE FLOW

To walk in this kind of divine creativity, consider these intentional rhythms:

- Write the Vision–Habakkuk 2:2 says it clearly: clarity grows when vision is written. Journals become blueprints.
- Surrender the Blueprint–Proverbs 3:5–6 reminds us: don't just plan, partner. Let God refine your direction.
- Start Small–Don't wait for a perfect moment. Begin. God breathes on movement.
- Silence Fear–Fear chokes creativity. But trust in God loosens its grip. Speak faith until boldness returns.

- Celebrate the Progress–Just like David remembered past victories before facing Goliath, you can gain courage by recalling your wins.

What Happens When You Shift?

- You stop seeing creativity as a personal effort and start treating it as a divine assignment.
- You no longer chase ideas—you receive them.
- You find joy in the process because you're building not just for success but for impact.

Reflection Prompt:

- What one creative idea have you put on pause because it felt too big or uncertain?
- How can you invite God into that space today—and let Him co-create something new with you?

CHRISTIANITY VS LEGALISM

Step into grace-filled freedom...

Discover the freedom Jesus offers—not through rules, but through heart transformation.

CHAPTER 8

CHRISTIANITY VS LEGALISM: EMBRACING TRUE FREEDOM

"For the message of the Cross is seen as foolishness by those who are perishing, yet to us who are being saved, it embodies the power of God." —1 Corinthians 1:18 (NIV)

THE DAY I WAS DENIED ENTRY INTO A CHURCH

It was my cousin's wedding - day of joy, unity, and family celebration. My husband, brother, and I had traveled to Nigeria to attend. Dressed for the occasion and full of excitement, we arrived at the church…only to be turned away.

At the entrance, an usher looked me over and asked, "No head covering?" Before I could respond, she made it clear: without a scarf, I wouldn't be allowed in.

We stood there, under the sweltering sun, as the ceremony carried on without us. Not because we were disruptive or late. Not because we weren't family. But because of a missing scarf. The rule, perhaps wellintended, felt more like a gate than guidance, and the deeper wound wasn't about tradition—it was the absence of grace.

WHEN RULES REPLACE RELATIONSHIP

Legalism thrives where rules take precedence over people. It focuses on appearance rather than heart, on behavior over transformation. It builds fences God never asked us to make.

Yes, God is holy. Yes, He values order and principle. But Jesus didn't die for rituals—He died for a relationship. And He constantly challenged the religious leaders of His day for prioritizing traditions over truth and regulations over redemption.

THE PROBLEM ISN'T ORDER—IT'S THE ABSENCE OF GRACE

The order is good. God is not chaotic. He is consistent, just, and righteous. Scripture reminds us He "does not change like shifting shadows" (James 1:17). But order without grace is bondage. Discipline without love is abuse.

I couldn't help but wonder if we had arrived with someone famous or influential, would an exception have been made? Jesus warned about this exact hypocrisy. The

Pharisees were praised for their knowledge of the law, but condemned for misapplying it.

They "tie up heavy, cumbersome loads and put them on other people's shoulders," Jesus said, "but they are not willing to lift a finger to move them" (Matthew 23:4). It wasn't their reverence He rebuked—it was their rigidity.

GRACE THAT CONFRONTS WITHOUT CONDEMNING

The woman caught in adultery should have been stoned according to the law. But when Jesus knelt and wrote in the dirt, He turned judgment into mercy. "Let the one without sin cast the first stone," he said. One by one, the accusers left. Grace remained.

When He healed a crippled woman on the Sabbath, the religious elite were outraged. But Jesus replied, "Shouldn't this daughter of Abraham be set free?" (Luke 13:16). For Jesus, people were never interruptions to His ministry—they were the ministry.

FREEDOM OVER FEAR

Legalism whispers, "Do more to be accepted." Jesus declares, "Come as you are—I've already made the way." True Christianity isn't rooted in performance but in presence—the presence of a Savior who bore our shame, fulfilled the law, and offered grace to the very ones who had broken it.

Yes, holiness matters. But holiness comes from love, not fear. When you realize you're deeply loved, obedience becomes a joy, not a burden. You desire to honor the One who rescued you, not out of obligation, but out of devotion.

A BETTER WITNESS

As believers, we're called to reflect not just the truth of Christ but also His tenderness. The way we represent Him—especially to those still exploring faith—matters deeply.

Let's ask: *Is our faith drawing people in—or driving them away?*

What Happens When You Shift?
- You exchange fear-based obedience for grace-filled transformation.
- You stop policing others and start walking with them.
- You reflect Jesus, not just in doctrine, but in demeanor.

Reflection Prompt:

- Where have you let pressure, rules, or appearances replace your intimacy with God?
- What would it look like to walk in the kind of grace you long to receive—and to extend that same grace to others?

THE DISCIPLINE OF DILIGENCE

Ready to move from stuck to steady? Here you'll find the tools to choose consistency over chaos—and build something lasting.

CHAPTER 9

THE DISCIPLINE OF DILIGENCE: OVERCOMING IDLENESS FOR GROWTH

"Go to the ant, you sluggard; consider its ways and be wise! It has no commander, no overseer or ruler, yet it stores its provisions in summer and gathers its food at harvest." — *Proverbs 6:6–8 (NIV)*

WHEN TOO MANY IDEAS BECOME TOO LITTLE ACTION

I once felt crushed—not by a lack of vision, but by an overload of it. The to-do list seemed endless, each task significant, each calling meaningful. And yet, whenever I sat down, I froze. The more I wrote, the more discouraged I became. I found myself whispering, "There's just too much."

That's when my sister-in-law spoke truth gently but firmly: "Your mind is overflowing, but structure is weak."

Months later, Lady VJ said something that cracked me

open: "Take one bite at a time. Work until that bite is fully swallowed before reaching for the next."

Suddenly, the wisdom I preached felt personal. I'd been advising others to start small, but I hadn't built the habit for myself. I share this not from a pedestal, but from a place of humility because every creative mind battles with overwhelm. And structure isn't the enemy—it's the pathway to freedom.

A WHISPER THAT CHANGED MY PACE

It was a quiet, almost forgettable afternoon—until a frail patient whispered something I'll never forget. We had been discussing his life, his writings, and the numerous ideas he had hoped to publish one day. Then, with tears in his eyes, he said, "I waited too long. I thought I had more time."

It wasn't regret that struck me most—it was the weight of unrealized potential. He had the vision, the language, the wisdom...but not the urgency. And now, the ideas that could've shaped others were trapped in the "whatifs" of delay.

That moment taught me a powerful truth: it's not the size of the vision that matters—it's the pace of your obedience. Diligence isn't about rushing; it's about moving with purpose while there's still time.

IDLENESS STEALS FROM OUR FUTURE

We often think idleness is apparent lounging, disengaged, doing nothing. But sometimes, idleness wears a disguise. It masks itself as planning, endless preparation, or "waiting for confirmation." But the truth? Hesitation, primarily when rooted in fear or perfectionism, is still a thief.

Scripture doesn't call the lazy person wicked—it calls them unwise. Proverbs 6 says the ant has no ruler, yet it stores for the future. That kind of wisdom doesn't wait for a perfect moment—it works diligently while it can.

Every time we postpone purpose, we give the enemy space to plant doubt. Every delay in obedience becomes a detour from impact. And if we're not careful, we'll wake up one day having built a life that looks busy but lacks fruit.

HARD WORK VS. DILIGENCE

Hard work is good, but it can be chaotic without a strategy. You can work tirelessly and still feel stuck if your efforts aren't aligned. Diligence is different. It's thoughtful. It's intentional. It's consistent, even when the spark is gone.

Think about Nehemiah. He didn't just charge into Jerusalem with excitement—he inspected the ruins, prayed for strategy, assigned responsibilities, and remained undistracted by critics. His diligence built what others only talked about.

In nature, people like Thomas Edison or Colonel Sanders faced countless rejections. But it wasn't genius that brought their ideas to life—it was grit. They didn't quit after the 5th or 50th failure. That's diligence: refusing to surrender the vision when it feels slow or unseen.

HOW TO CULTIVATE DILIGENCE

1. Start small–Break your big vision into doable steps.
2. Treat time as sacred–Unplug distractions. Use tools like the Pomodoro Technique.
3. Invite accountability–Faithful partners call you out and cheer you on.
4. Celebrate wins–Acknowledging progress fuels future action.

THE HARVEST OF CONSISTENCY

Proverbs 13:4 reminds us: "The diligent will get their fill." Comparison fades when you stay faithful. You don't have to be the smartest or most connected. You must be consistent. The steady, humble, disciplined person often finishes the race.

What Happens When You Shift?

- Overwhelm gives way to clarity and actionable steps.

- Fear of delay transforms into momentum and progress.
- You become someone who builds, not just starts—something significant.

Reflection Prompt:

- What small action can you take today to move forward?
- Who can you invite to hold you accountable and celebrate with you?

FAITHFUL LIVING: SUCCESS & INCREASE

Redefine success—Kingdom style...

This chapter shows you how purpose-driven living outlasts fame and fortune.

CHAPTER 10

FAITHFUL LIVING: THE PATH TO SUCCESS & INCREASE

"In all your ways submit to him, and he will make your paths straight." – Proverbs 3:6 (NIV) *"If you are faithful in little things, you will be faithful in large ones."*
—Luke 16:10 (NLT)

THE DAY SUCCESS WAS REDEFINED FOR ME

Earlier this year, I attended a Success Summit where my mentor, Lady VJ, shared a truth that resonated deeply with me. She said, "Success is not about how much money you're making. It's about knowing what solutions you carry and what problems you are uniquely designed to solve. When people begin to recognize the answers you bring and seek you out for them—that's success." Her words took me back to a moment two years before I opened my clinic. I was stuck in traffic, heart heavy under the weight of uncertainty, when I felt that gentle nudge: "Do you see all these buildings? They're not just brick and mortar—they represent solutions."

Not every structure solves a problem, but every genuine business I saw existed to meet a need. A daycare supports working parents. A tire shop solves mobility issues. Then it hit me: "Your clinic will also be a solution, not just a business but a place of healing."

That realization redefined success for me. It's not about how grand your dream is—it's about the need it fulfills and the lives it impacts. Faithfulness to addressing that need brings rewards far beyond recognition or revenue.

WHEN PURPOSE OUTWEIGHS PROFIT

It's easy to chase wealth, influence, or applause. But when those become our motivations, we often end up feeling empty. True success isn't a paycheck—it's a purpose.

Take Joshua 1:8: success is tied to meditating on God's Word—integrating it into daily life. When our goals align with God's path (Proverbs 3:6), peace and impact follow, even if the world's applause doesn't.

THE PRODIGAL'S PATH: RESTORATION AS ACHIEVEMENT

Most of us know the story of the prodigal son, leaving, losing, then returning. But it's not just a tale of forgiveness, it's a blueprint for maturity.

He returned not with success, but surrender. And that

shift mattered more than gold. In modern times, consider John Newton, whose transformation from slave trader to author of "Amazing Grace" became more than a career—it became a legacy of redemption. Real success often begins with return, not ascent.

STEWARDSHIP: MONEY, TIME, AND INFLUENCE

God entrusts us with resources, but they are not meant for hoarding; they are meant for multiplication and distribution. Ruth stayed with Naomi not out of obligation, but out of heart alignment, an act that not only blessed her but also shaped generations to come.

Truett Cathy, founder of Chick-fil-A, built a kingdom-conscious brand by closing on Sundays and giving back weekly, showing us that business can bless people more than just profit.

THE BALANCE OF BUSYNESS AND BEING

In the busyness of life, the tragedy isn't doing too much, it's doing everything but the right things. Mary and Martha teach us that sitting quietly with Jesus is sometimes the most challenging, most productive work (Luke 10:38-42). Even modern leaders, CEOs, and entrepreneurs share that without rest and reflection, success dims into daredevil burnout.

Elon Musk himself has admitted the cost of relentless hustle. The real success? It's the ability to manage tasks without losing sight of and damaging relationships.

LIVING SUCCESS IN THE EVERYDAY

True success isn't just a firework—it's a slow-burning torch. It's found in asking daily, "Does this align with your path, God?" and faithfully doing small things—whether returning calls, mentoring a colleague, or serving a neighbour. When we steward our time, talent, and treasure with integrity, small acts become legacies. Joseph's journey reminds us that faithfulness in every dark corridor prepared him for a life of influence and blessing.

What Happens When You Shift?

- Purpose reigns: No more chasing applause—you're anchored in calling.
- You become a multiplier: Stewardship opens channels for impact, not just income.
- Balance comes: Busyness becomes a tool, not your identity.

Reflection Prompt:

- In what area of your life do you need to align your efforts with God's direction?
- What small habit (like generosity, words of encouragement, Sabbath rest) can you commit to this week that honors purpose over performance?

PERSISTENCE & PROFIT

Grab hold of faith-filled follow-through...Hard work carries a reward. Stick around—this chapter equips you to persevere and achieve a breakthrough.

CHAPTER 11

PERSISTENCE & PROFIT: THRIVING THROUGH FAITHFULNESS

"All hard work brings profit, but mere talk leads only to poverty." —Proverbs 12:23, NIV

"She recognizes that her trading yields profit and her lamp remains lit throughout the night." —Proverbs 31:18, NIV

THE NURSE WHO REFUSED TO QUIT

I once supported a nurse who had failed her LPN board exam not once, but five times. Each attempt chipped away at her confidence. She wondered whether she was suited for the profession. But I reminded her: "You're only one attempt away from success." Drawing inspiration from Thomas Edison's 999 failures before the lightbulb, she tried again and again. On the sixth attempt, she passed. Then came her RN, then her BSN. Her transformation wasn't just measured in titles—it was faith in action. Her persistence didn't promise ease, but it guaranteed growth, and that growth ignited her transformation.

LIFE DESIGNED FOR GROWTH

Faithful profit in God's economy isn't just about bank numbers, it's about multiplication: of character, impact, and spiritual fruit. In Matthew 25:14-30, the parable of the talents clearly shows that God expects us to invest what He has given us. The master praises the servants who multiplied their share, not because they had more, but because they were faithful.

Your gifts—spiritual, emotional, and relational are seeds to sow. When nurtured, they produce not just for you, but for your community. Like a gardener tending to every seed with care, your consistent effort reaches far beyond the surface.

THE POWER OF PERSISTENCE

Persistence is the secret weapon of the faithful. Consider Bartimaeus, the blind man in Mark 10:46-52. Crowds tried to silence him, yet he shouted louder: "Son of David, have mercy on me!" His relentless faith earned him healing.

Remember the Canaanite woman in Matthew 15:21-28. Rejected and overlooked, she didn't quit until Jesus responded. Her humble persistence showcased that even crumbs of grace are enough.

These biblical giants didn't scheme or demand—they persisted. And their persistence was rewarded. Obedience and character were strengthened in the process.

PRACTICAL STEPS FOR FAITHFUL GROWTH

1. Identify & Activate What You Have

Take stock of your talents and resources. You don't need more, you need intentionality in what you already possess.

2. Break Big Goals into Small Wins

Overwhelm often keeps us stuck. Choose one thing you can do today; write one page, make one call, send one email. Remember that consistency compounds.

3. Find Your Support Circle

Surround yourself with encouragers and accountability partners. A community that prays, celebrates, and challenges helps keep your lamp burning.

4. Celebrate Every Milestone

Small wins fuel the journey. Just as David celebrated past victories over a lion and a bear before Goliath, speak your achievements aloud and trust God's next step.

5. Refuse to Quit

When discouragement knocks, lean on Scripture and your support system. Trials don't define you—they refine you. And breakthroughs come to those anchored in faith.

What Happens When You Shift?

- You stop measuring success by effort alone and begin seeing transformation through faithful cultivation.

- You no longer fear setbacks; instead, you use them as fuel for forward momentum.

- You become a steward of persistence, someone who doesn't just start but finishes, knowing every seed sown in faith brings a harvest in time.

Reflection Prompt:

- What gift or opportunity are you neglecting because it seems too small or imperfect?

- How can you take one meaningful step, without waiting for more resources, validation, or perfect conditions?

- Who will walk with you, pray for you, and remind you of your purpose when you feel like stopping?

THE GRAVEYARD OF GREATNESS

Time to unearth your potential...

No more playing small. This chapter empowers you to step out before regret sets in.

CHAPTER 12

THE GRAVEYARD OF GREATNESS: HOW TO AVOID WASTED POTENTIAL

"To those who use well what they are given, even more, will be given, and they will have an abundance. But from those who do nothing, even what little they have will be taken away." —Matthew 25:29 (NLT)

THE DAY I REALIZED POTENTIAL ISN'T FOREVER

I remember listening to a YouTube message by the Late Dr. Myles Munroe, that day when he dropped the truth bomb: "The wealthiest place on earth is not the oil fields... It's the graveyard." He paused, scanning the crowd, then spoke on—"Because there lie the unwritten books, the unpainted art, the unsung songs, the unrealized dreams."

That moment felt like a spotlight on my soul. I thought about my ideas—some scribbled in notebooks, some only whispered in prayer—and I asked myself: Will I bury them, or will I plant them to grow?

REVEALING HIDDEN POTENTIAL

You are not here by accident. Psalm 139:14 reminds us we are "fearfully and wonderfully made." That means your voice, your calling, your unique burdens—they all matter.

But fear, comparison, or perfectionism can make us ignore God's fingerprints on our lives. We see someone else walking in purpose and think, They're ready—I'm not. Sometimes the sobbing inside me whispered: I'm too late. But God gently reminded me: Your story still has chapters left.

One patient I met, a quiet schoolteacher, never stood on a podium. Yet every week, she poured life into her students—not for applause, but from a deep, unspoken commitment. That kind of gift matters in eternity.

CREATING A LEGACY THAT OUTLASTS SELF

Legacy isn't reserved for the famous. It's quietly woven through consistency, loyalty, and love. The Bible calls it "planting and watering," and promises that we'll be rewarded for our labor, even the unseen. Take the Sunday school teacher who repeats the same lesson with care or the volunteer who cleans the church after service—no one thanks them, but God sees. Legacy isn't flashy; it's the small decisions made with great love. Those unseen stones become the foundation on which others build.

OVERCOMING THE BARRIER TO EXECUTION

Ideas are beautiful, until they remain only in our minds. Execution is where dreams meet reality. That moment when you think, I'll write the first page this morning. You don't need to have everything figured out. You just need to show up again and again.

One friend shared: "My book was terrible. But I turned to the first chapter anyway." It became a catalyst. That single act of momentum broke the cycle of self-doubt. Consistency builds competence. It grows grit. It transforms your whispers into a witness.

EXCUSES VS. KINGDOM COURAGE

Excuses sound spiritual, I'm not ready. I'll wait for the next season. And yet, they steal better seasons. Moses stuttered. Gideon felt small. Mary is a teenage girl. None of them had all the credentials. But each obeyed. In contrast, our excuses often feel safe...until we're holding ashes in our hands.

God has equipped your next step—even if it's small. He

calls it courage, but it often looks like a trembling foot lifted in faith.

LEGACY IS BUILT IN QUIET MOMENTS

We live in a loud culture, but history is shaped by whispered commitments—in hospital rooms, on school benches, and in prayer closets.

Think of that Sunday school teacher continuing week after week. The parent sacrifices time to sit and listen, and the friend who shows up.

Those off-the-record choices matter. Those seeds of faithfulness become forests of courage, love, and integrity. Even if no one writes about them, heaven isn't watching silently.

What Happens When You Shift?

- You awaken what was dormant, giving your gifts room to breathe.
- You see legacy as both loud and quiet, extending beyond fame to faithfulness.
- You trade perfection for presence, learning to move imperfectly but persistently.
- You release excuses, choosing courageous steps over safety.

- You live as a steward, knowing every small act matters in the Kingdom tapestry.

Reflection Prompt:

- What gift have you kept in the dark? Will today be the day you let it breathe?
- What small, faithful act are you called to in your hidden places?
- How will you choose courage over comfort this week?

BEYOND SURVIVAL

Get ready to thrive...

Busy isn't the same as blessed. Discover how alignment surpasses hustle and brings soul-deep peace.

CHAPTER 13

BEYOND SURVIVAL: THRIVING IN GOD'S CALLING

"Blessed is the one who perseveres under trial because, having stood the test, that person will receive the crown of life that the Lord has promised to those who love him."
—James 1:12 (NIV)

THE MORNING I REALIZED I WAS JUST SURVIVING

It was one of those mornings when everything felt urgent. Emails, patient charts, groceries, family schedules, church prep, and clinic tasks, yet a restless hollowness set into my soul. I wasn't asleep at the wheel; I was driving full speed on autopilot. For the first time, I admitted it out loud: I'm surviving, not living. The busyness felt like movement, but my spirit whispered that I wasn't in step with His rhythm anymore.

REDEFINING FREEDOM: CHOOSING PURPOSE OVER PRODUCTIVITY

We live in a culture where doing more is applauded, but God often whispers, "What matters most?" Elijah, after doing incredible things, found himself running scared and depleted. At Mount Horeb, God didn't speak in rockshaking majesty, but in a gentle whisper (1 Kings 19). That whisper revealed the truth: freedom isn't about permission to do it all—it's about the wisdom to do what matters. Are you doing everything you can, or everything you should?

TIME STEWARDSHIP: DISCOVERING "ME TIME" IN A HECTIC WORLD

Time is God's precious gift. But when your calendar bursts at the seams, stillness feels irresponsible. That's a lie. Jesus often withdrew not to escape, but to be alone (Luke 5:16). The early church made room for worship, teaching, service, and generosity (Acts 2:42-47). Richness wasn't measured in activity, it was measured in depth. Stillness isn't indulgence, it's devotion. It's where your heart remembers who's holding your schedule.

ALIGNMENT THAT OPENS NEW DOORS

Real productivity happens when your activity aligns with your calling. Peter fished all night and caught nothing—until he obeyed a whisper from Jesus, and the nets brimmed (Luke 5).

Joseph's journey—a betrayal, prison, and invisibility prepared him for a moment that only he could fulfill. He wasn't delayed; he was refined.

What if your current season is less about busyness and more about becoming—becoming the person who can steward greater things?

THRIVING IN QUIET OBEDIENCE

Thriving doesn't always look like success. Sometimes, it seems like steadfast faith.

I think of a woman I once met who lost her husband, then both children. There were no miracles, yet she kept showing up—praying, trusting, loving without fanfare. Her story wasn't marked by rescue, it was marked by quiet resilience.

That is true thriving, not in outcome, but in obedience.

What Happens When You Shift?

- You pause the autopilot and begin to listen to God's rhythm again.
- You replace frantic doing with aligned being, discovering purpose rooted in His presence.
- You guard sacred margins—spaces for prayer, rest, and reflection.
- You experience unseen transformation—quiet growth that prepares you for unseen elevation.

Reflection Prompt:

- What part of your day feels rushed but not rich?
- Where could you pause to align with purpose instead of productivity?
- What small margin can you create this week to invite God's whisper—and what might He say?

BUILDING A LEGACY

Start seeing your ripple impact...

Legacy hearkens beyond you. Let this chapter help you raise tomorrow's world leaders.

CHAPTER 14

BUILDING A LEGACY: TURNING PURPOSE INTO DAILY ACTION

"A good man leaves an inheritance for his children's children, but a sinner's wealth is stored up for the righteous." —Proverbs 13:22 (NIV)

A LEGACY THAT ECHOES BEYOND TODAY

I remember sitting with a teacher I'd cared for in my clinic for nearly two decades—someone who believed her influence had run its course. She despaired that 18 years of classroom work might never leave a mark beyond dusty halls and forgotten lesson plans.

Yet on her desk lay a dusty application for her doctorate in education. Tears welled as she confessed, "What if it's too late? What if my kids pay the price?"

We prayed together, and I reminded her that legacy isn't handed down, it's woven day by day. She courageously went back to school. Four years later, she emerged with Dr. before her name. She didn't just lift her family—she set a new trajectory for them. Her children graduated debt-free and are now pursuing graduate studies themselves. Her story reminds us: legacy is created by choosing faith over fear, one courageous decision at a time. Proverbs 13:22 isn't just good advice—it's a heartbeat: our daily choices echo beyond our years.

SEEDS OF IMPACT: THE QUIET ROOMS OF INFLUENCE

Legacy is often built in places where applause never reaches. Not everyone will preach on platforms or run global ministries. Sometimes, legacy takes root in the quiet rooms where faithfulness is the only spotlight. I remember a woman in my old church, we called her "Auntie Joy." She wasn't a preacher or a title leader, but she taught Sunday school for over 20 years. Her classroom was tucked behind the main sanctuary, painted in colors that had long since faded. But every Saturday, she prepared her lessons with such care.

On Sundays, she welcomed each child with joy in her voice and warmth in her eyes. She wasn't just teaching Bible stories; she was planting seeds of identity and hope in young hearts. Many of those children grew up to become leaders, creatives, parents, and even pastors—and to this day, they still talk about Auntie Joy's impact.

There was also Brother Tunde, the man who cleaned

the church. You'd find him there before the sun rose, sweeping the floors, setting up chairs, and fixing whatever was broken. He never expected thanks, and he never asked for a platform. But I'll never forget how he once comforted a woman who came in crying, thinking no one noticed her pain. It wasn't the pastor who first reached her, it was the janitor who listened. These are the kinds of lives that remind us: legacy doesn't need lights, it needs love.

WEALTH, WISDOM, AND THE HEART'S INVESTMENT

True legacy isn't just about material inheritance, it's about how we steward what God has given us and the people our lives touch along the way. Take the teacher I mentioned earlier—now Dr. Groshan. Her story didn't end with a degree. After earning her doctorate, she began advocating for underserved schools in her district. She set up tutoring programs, supported first-generation college students, and inspired fellow educators to dream again. She didn't just climb the ladder—she pulled others up with her. That's what it looks like to invest beyond yourself.

And then there's the story of Chadwick Boseman. Many knew him for his influential on-screen roles, especially in Black Panther, but what most didn't realize until after his passing was that he had been battling cancer throughout much of his career. Even amid his pain, he chose to serve. He visited children in hospitals, gave commencement speeches, and carried himself with quiet strength. His legacy wasn't about fame—it was about faithfulness to purpose, even under pressure.

TAKING A STEP TODAY

Legacy isn't built in a day—it's cultivated one intentional act at a time. You don't need a grand stage or a famous title. You need a willing heart and consistent faithfulness.

1. Who are you influencing?
2. What value are you offering?
3. Where can you volunteer time or resources today?

What Happens When You Shift?

- You stop running on approval and start cultivating character.
- Your daily decisions become seeds, watered by prayer, purpose, and caring relationships.
- Your investments court eternity, leaving behind wisdom, hope, and resilience.

Reflection Prompt:

- What daily choice can you make today that reflects your heart's deepest convictions?
- If you could leave one lesson behind, what would it be—and how can your actions today begin that teaching?

MASTERING LIFE'S SEASONS

Seasoned for a reason...

Pressure forms diamonds. Abundance is a trust test. Embrace the process and let God shape you.

CHAPTER 15

MASTERING LIFE'S SEASONS: THRIVING IN EVERY STAGE

"We also glory in our sufferings, because we know that suffering produces perseverance; perseverance, character; and character, hope." Romans 5:3-4 (NIV)

FROM HOSPITAL ROOMS TO BREAKTHROUGHS: WHEN SEASONS SHIFT YOU UNEXPECTEDLY

It was well after midnight when the call came—my dear friend's daughter had been rushed into emergency surgery. As I drove through the quiet streets, I whispered prayers, leaned into the promises of Scripture, and braced my heart. My friend, a woman who had poured herself out to others without hesitation, now needed to receive. By morning, the girl was on the path to recovery, but something deeper stirred. Reflecting on the night, my friend shared, "That night broke me, but it also built me. Instead of asking 'why me?' I asked, 'What now, Lord?'"

In that moment, pain became more than just something to

endure—it became an invitation to trust God's unfolding plan. Life won't always align with our schedules, but we do get to choose how we walk through what comes.

LIFE'S TAPESTRY: EVERY SEASON HAS PURPOSE

Life is like a richly woven quilt—some squares full of vibrant, joyful hues; others darkened by sorrow or uncertainty. Ecclesiastes 7:14 reminds us that both sides hold purpose: seasons of hardship shape our resilience, while seasons of plenty grow our gratitude.

Take Joseph, for example—a young man betrayed by his brothers, sold into slavery, and imprisoned. Yet each step of that painful journey was preparing him for leadership and provision in Egypt. And Esther, an orphan raised in obscurity, later found the courage to intercede for her people—her quiet season of preparation positioned her perfectly for a moment of destiny.

These stories remind us: it's not always about the destination, but about how each season shapes our strength, insight, and readiness for what comes next.

TURNING PAIN INTO PURPOSE

Justice sometimes whispers, "Why me?" but God often responds, "Watch how I turn this around." After a devastating fire burned his initial restaurant, Chick-fil-

A's founder, Truett Cathy, rebuilt and birthed a legacy business that became a ministry for many. His pain led to purpose.

Consider Dr. Nicole Robinson Caillier. She began as a nursing aide, worked her way into management, only to be unexpectedly let go. Rather than retreat, she launched a healthcare staffing empire—and now mentors countless professionals across the country. Her setback became a sacred redirection.

Their lives remind us: when one door closes, it's often God's hand gently nudging open another one filled with more profound impact, meaning, and legacy.

NAVIGATING ABUNDANCE WITH GRACE

Prosperity can be as deceptively challenging as hardship. When things go well, it's easy to drift—comfort can numb us, success can swell our pride, and blessing can lull us into complacency. Yet, as Psalm 23 beautifully paints, "Even though I walk through the valley... You prepare a table before me." Abundance isn't just a gift, it's trust.

Picture a farmer after a plentiful harvest. He doesn't stash away everything—he shares it generously, saves for seasons ahead, and invests in what nurtures his community and land. That posture of cheerful generosity is what God invites us into: sharing resources, time, and talents in ways that bless others and multiply impact.

Remember David—when the Ark returned to Jerusalem, he danced before God with all his might (2 Samuel 6). Not to seek attention, but to honor the source of every blessing.

Without that spirit of humility and generosity, abundance can trip us into idolatry, where our possessions begin to possess us. But when gratitude, wisdom, generosity, and celebration anchor our hearts, prosperity becomes a divine tool, not a trap.

WISDOM IN THE IN-BETWEEN

Those middle seasons, the ones that feel stagnant or unremarkable, are quietly sacred. They're not just pauses; they're workshops for our soul. Think of Esther again—with weeks or even months of waiting and seeking God before stepping into palaces and a pivotal season of influence (Esther 4). Or Moses, who spent forty years tending sheep in the desert before God called him out from a burning bush.

In these times, who we become matters more than what we accomplish. Patience deepens, character is refined, and clarity takes root. Called "in-between seasons," they're divine intervals for preparation and alignment, not empty gaps.

These seasons invite us to listen: to God's quiet voice, the stirrings in our hearts, and the hopes He's woven into us. They are seasons of quiet formation—time to surrender our timelines and learn from the Author of our story.

THRIVING ISN'T A DESTINATION

Often, we treat thriving like a mountaintop we'll reach once everything aligns, when finances are stable, relationships are healthy, and ministry or work feels abundant. But the heart of thriving isn't a place, it's a posture.

Thriving is choosing peace amid uncertainty, joy in the mundane, and faith when the answer hasn't come yet. It's anchoring your soul not in the absence of storms, but in the One who holds you within them.

Paul was in chains when he wrote letters that each followed logic but were saturated with hope and encouragement. Hannah, who prayed fervently while childless, brought her open heart as worship before her answer arrived. Those are thriving stories—not of perfect circumstances, but of enduring faith.

Thriving isn't flashy. It's faith filled. It's a daily choice to abide, trust, and respond, knowing that true flourishing looks more like faithful presence than finished perfection.

What Happens When You Shift?

- You begin to see seasons not as obstacles to endure, but as opportunities to grow and prepare.
- You become alert to lessons hidden in both struggle and quiet blessing.
- You steward every stage with trust, leaning into challenge, and giving in abundance.
- You root your confidence not in your environment, but in a God whose character never changes.

Reflection Prompt:

- What season are you in right now— challenge, abundance, or somewhere in between?
- How might God be shaping your heart in this moment?
- What resources—resilience, insight, rest— has He entrusted to you?
- How might you steward them in this season for greater impact?

THE POWER OF DISCIPLESHIP

It's your turn to pour out...

You've been mentored. Now it's time to mentor. Training leaders is your spiritual assignment.

CHAPTER 16

THE POWER OF DISCIPLESHIP: WALKING IN KINGDOM AUTHORITY

"Believe in the Lord your God, and you shall be established; believe in His prophets, and you shall prosper."
—*2 Chronicles 20:20 (KJV)*

WALKING WITH PURPOSE: MY MENTORS, MY GUIDES

From the moment I met Dr. Joy Jones in 2017, her life spoke louder than words. As a global minister, counselor, best-selling author, thriving businesswoman, and devoted mother, she wasn't accumulating titles, she was radiating obedience. I watched her life ripple with Kingdom resilience; it was clear that every part of her was surrendered to God.

I remember sitting across from her, pouring out my heart: dreams, business ideas, a vision that felt overwhelming. I felt tangled. Like I could do anything but couldn't do everything. That's when she shared wisdom I'll carry for a lifetime:

Life is like a house with many rooms... but you don't open them all at once. Ask God for your master key—your core purpose. Once you find that key, the right doors open in His timing. It grounded me. It simplified a confused mind.

Then came Lady VJ and her Lady School. Her mentorship wasn't just practical, it was powerful. She challenged me, sharpened me, and equipped me to walk in purpose with action, not just talk. It wasn't surfacelevel coaching; it was discipleship that ignited and propelled me.

Through these two women, I learned that discipleship isn't just about advice, it's about becoming. It's about who you are when you stand under godly counsel, and what you do with those lessons.

MORE THAN MOTIVATION: THE DEPTH OF DISCIPLESHIP

In an era where online platforms offer quick inspiration, what we need is spiritual formation, transformation that lasts. That's the heart of discipleship. Jesus didn't just speak from far away, He lived alongside His twelve disciples. He corrected them, empowered them, and released them to continue His work (see Matthew 28).

Consider Moses passing the mantle to Joshua. Or Elijah, mentoring Elisha while climbing heavenward on a fiery chariot ride. Or Paul guiding Timothy, pouring out decades of wisdom so Timothy could shepherd churches with confidence. These stories aren't ancient relics, they're blueprints for a legacy that spans generations.

Discipleship is the engine by which Kingdom influence doesn't fade, it multiplies. It's how faith becomes sustainable, not just sentimental.

WHAT DISCIPLESHIP DOES

Discipleship does more than inform, it transforms:
- It refines your identity and calling.
- It teaches submission to God's timing and process.
- It offers correction that builds, not breaks.
- It reminds us that trust outweighs hurry.

But here's the real beauty: discipleship isn't a one-way street. We're not just to receive; we're to give. Your story, your scars, your breakthroughs, they're not just yours. They become someone else's roadmap.

KINGDOM AUTHORITY IN MOTION

Imagine your life as a lantern passed from hand to hand. Discipleship hands light to others. In doing so, you walk in Kingdom authority rooted in faithfulness, humility, and multiplication, not hierarchy.

When you embrace a mentor's guidance, it shapes you. When you choose to pour what you've received into another, the light doesn't diminish—it multiplies.

What Happens When You Shift?

- You go from being inspired to being formed, and wisdom transforms into a lifestyle.
- You ordain your life not to follow trends, but to steward a divine calling.
- You become a carrier of transformation, not just a recipient.

Reflection Prompt:

- Who has God placed in your corner as a mentor?
- How can you honour their influence by stepping forward boldly and then doing the same for someone else?

EPILOGUE

You were created to lead, to influence, and to govern— not to hide in obscurity. God planted seeds of purpose within you, not to be hoarded, but to be shared. Imagine if innovators like Elon Musk or Steve Jobs had silenced their spark—we'd still be wondering what's possible. And what if Moses, Paul, or even Jesus had declined their call?

Your gifts carry healing, innovation, and hope to a world waiting for Kingdom-shifters like you. You are not designed to spectate, you are called to change the game. 1 Peter 2:9 reminds us:

"You are a chosen people, a royal priesthood... that you may declare the praises of Him who called you out of darkness into His wonderful light."

Royalty doesn't shrink; royalty steps into the centre.

YOUR SPARK WAS JUST THE START

This book was more than a read, it was a starting point:

- You've reclaimed spiritual and personal authority.
- You've overcome fear, excuses, and the lies that masquerade as wisdom.
- You've begun aligning your life with a higher calling and stepping into your sphere of influence.

The world is ready, not for another spectator, but for purposeful, bold leaders like you. God is raising a generation of Kingdom gatekeepers, and you're already at the vanguard.

RISE, RULE, REFLECT

Now, it's time. Step forward and reclaim your God-given power. You weren't made to drift—you were made to rule.

THIS IS NOT THE END. IT'S THE BEGINNING.

Growth is rarely linear. Transformation unfolds gradually, sometimes quietly, often in the underground. Whether you're in a season of clarity or still navigating the unknown, trust that God wastes nothing. Stay rooted. Stay expectant. Even now, your story is being written with greater purpose.

A PARTING ENCOURAGEMENT

May courage surge in your heart and wisdom guide your steps. May your faith remain steadfast as you fulfill the mission God has entrusted to you.

This moment is yours. The world is waiting. Rise, rule, and reflect His glory.

REFERENCES

Bible References (Digital Sources Only)

Holy Bible, King James Version. (1769). YouVersion Bible App (Original work published 1611). Retrieved from https://www.bible.com

Holy Bible, New International Version. (2011). Zondervan Study Bible (Digital Edition). Zondervan. Retrieved from https://www.biblegateway.com

Holy Bible, New Living Translation. (2015). Life Application Study Bible (Digital Edition). Tyndale House Publishers. Retrieved from https://www.biblegateway.com

Holy Bible, New Living Translation. (2024). Bible Gateway Online Edition. Zondervan. Retrieved from https://www.biblegateway.com

Books & Published Works

Barnes, B. (2020). Chadwick Boseman: A Remarkable Life. Little, Brown and Company.

Cathy, S. T. (2002). Eat Mor Chikin: Inspire More People. Looking Glass Books.

Isaacson, W. (2011). Steve Jobs. Simon & Schuster.

Munroe, M. (2003). Understanding Your Potential: Discovering the Hidden You. Destiny Image Publishers.

Stross, R. (2007). The Wizard of Menlo Park: How Thomas Edison Invented the Modern World. Crown.

Vance, A. (2015). Elon Musk: Tesla, SpaceX, and the Quest for a Fantastic Future. HarperCollins.

Online Articles & Web Sources

Forbes. (2023, March 10). Chadwick Boseman's Inspiring Legacy of Purpose. Retrieved from https://www.forbes.com

Harvard Health Publishing. (2022, June 15). How Stress Affects Your Body. Harvard Medical School. Retrieved from https://www.health.harvard.edu

TED. (2014, October). Nick Vujicic: Overcoming Hopelessness [Video]. YouTube. Retrieved from https://www.youtube.com/watch?v=ckIB1yfo1A

www.ingramcontent.com/pod-product-compliance
Lightning Source LLC
Chambersburg PA
CBHW070509100426
42743CB00010B/1796